# At the POWWOW

by Winston White
illustrated by Reggie Holladay

Editorial Offices: Glenview, Illinois • Parsippany, New Jersey • New York, New York
Sales Offices: Needham, Massachusetts • Duluth, Georgia • Glenview, Illinois
Coppell, Texas • Ontario, California • Mesa, Arizona

"Gram, tell me again why we go to the powwow," said Ben.

"The powwow is a place to celebrate with song and dance," said Gram. "We meet with our family and friends. It's a chance for young people to hear our language and the stories of the elders. Get ready. We don't want to be late!"

Dad and Mom were already in their powwow outfits. Dad was dressed for the men's traditional dance. His clothes were made of leather from a deer, called buckskin. His outfit was decorated with fringe and white bones. He wore two feathers on his head. The feathers would twirl when Dad danced.

Mom wore a jingle dress. Her dress had hundreds of small, metal cones on it. They were in a special pattern. The jingles would shake and make a beautiful ringing sound when Mom danced.

They set off for the powwow once
the family was ready. The powwow
grounds were filled with people.

The dance area was set up as a circle.
A second circle was outside the dance
area. The drum groups, dancers, and
families would sit there.

Ben heard the drums begin the opening song. The dancers, elders, and children got in line. They all marched into the dance area. Ben and Gram danced along with everyone else.

Ben watched the men. "Gram, tell me about the drums," said Ben.

"The drums are the heartbeat of our people," Gram said. "The men join their voices with the drums to make songs. Listen, Ben, they are singing in our language."

Soon it was time for the different dances to begin. Ben and Gram watched from the stands. They saw Dad in the men's traditional dance. Later, they watched as Mom joined the jingle dress dancers.

When Ben saw the little boy dancers, he said, "Gram, I want to do those dances at the powwow next year."

Gram and Ben looked around the booths. They heard the clattering of pots and pans as people cooked food. Some people were selling crafts.

Ben saw a silver bracelet. "Gram, may I borrow some money? I'd like to buy that bracelet for Mom."

"Sure, what a nice idea," said Gram.

Gram, Ben, Mom, and Dad sat down to eat. Ben gave Mom the bracelet.

"Thank you, Ben!" said Mom, as she hugged him.

They finished their meal at the powwow. Ben felt happy about this special family day.

# The Green Corn Festival

Some Native Americans celebrate a holiday called the Green Corn Festival. It takes place when the Moon is full and the first crop of corn is ready for harvest. The holiday is a time of thanksgiving for the corn crops. Once the first corn is picked, people dance, sing, and eat. Many of the foods are made from corn, such as corn soup, corn bread, and corn tortillas.